DEPRESSION

MINNESOTA IN THE THIRTIES

DEPRESSION

MINNESOTA IN THE THIRTIES

D. JEROME TWETON

NORTH DAKOTA INSTITUTE FOR REGIONAL STUDIES
FARGO • 1981

ALSO BY D. JEROME TWETON

The Marquis de Morès: Dakota Capitalist, French Nationalist

The Years of Despair: North Dakota in The Depression
(with Daniel F. Rylance)

North Dakota: The Heritage of A People
(with Theodore Jelliff)

"In Union There Is Strength:" The North Dakota Labor Movement and The United Brotherhood of Carpenters and Joiners

ISBN 0-911042-25-3
PRINTED IN THE U.S.A. BY KNIGHT PRINTING, FARGO

CONTENTS

To
Robert Poole Wilkins

All photographs in this book are used with the permission of
THE MINNESOTA HISTORICAL SOCIETY

I ". . . MILLIONS OF PEOPLE ARE DESPERATE": ECONOMIC CHAOS

John Bosch's stomach churned with anxiety as he saw his neighbors lose their farms and watched his crop sell for a few cents a bushel. Hard working and dedicated to his land, he could not tolerate the sight of the despair around him. The Reverend George Mecklenburg sat at his desk in his downtown Minneapolis church. His heart wrenched as he witnessed the daily parade of hungry, unemployed people pass through the shadow of the cross. He knew that the 20,000 who walked the streets without jobs had devoured the city's relief funds. The gloom on their faces tormented his conscience. Governor Floyd B. Olson impatiently paced back and forth in his office. Each report which crossed his desk roused his sensitive compassion for the well-being of the people. His state was under siege: farmers were ready to strike; restless urban workers demanded immediate relief; unemployment on the iron range pressed toward 70 percent. The worsening condition of his state made him angry. It was 1932. The depression had struck Minnesota.

The 1920s had not been generous to farmers. World War One had brought artificially high prices which most farmers thought would become normal. All-out war production, unfavorable tariffs, and technological change soon produced farm surpluses which drove down prices. For example, in July 1920 wheat sold at Minneapolis for $2.96 a bushel. A year and a half later it tumbled to 92 cents. Throughout the 1920s the price fluctuated between 97 cents and $1.20. During the early months of the 1930s wheat plummeted to 36 cents, although crop failures and government regulation raised it to 70 cents in 1934. Other farm products suffered the same fate; by 1932 farmers were selling hogs for three cents a pound and milk for two cents a quart. Although deflation brought down all prices, farm prices fell more sharply, placing the farmer in a terrifying price squeeze. In 1932 and 1933 farm-mortgage foreclosures became commonplace; in 1933, 60 of every 1,000 farmers went bankrupt or lost their farms through foreclosures. With no control over his market, the farmer felt helpless. When drought or grasshoppers struck, he felt hopeless.

The inability of the Herbert Hoover administration to deal with the farmers' dilemma provoked members of the Farmers' Union into joining a more action-oriented organization, the Farmers' Holiday Association. On May 3, 1932, over 2,000 farmers from several states launched the Farmers' Holiday Association and selected the well-known Iowa Farmers' Union leader Milo Reno as its president. The Holiday Association's remedy was simple: hold back farm products until the farmer realized the cost of production. "Restore the farmer's purchasing power," declared Reno, "and you will re-establish an endless chain of prosperity and happiness in the country."

John Bosch, president of the Kandiyohi County Farmers' Union, emerged as the force behind the Farmers' Holiday Association in Minnesota. During May and June 1932 he visited most Minnesota counties, attempting to rally farmers to the new organization. On July 29 a convention of farmers from fifty counties convened at St. Cloud, organized the Minnesota Farmers' Holiday Association, and chose Bosch as its leader.

In early August the Iowa Holiday Association tried to force up milk prices in Sioux City by withholding all shipments. Farmers jammed the highways to blockade all milk trucks; drivers who resisted saw their milk spilled out over the road. Throughout August farmers succeeded in focusing national attention on their plight. In early September four governors — Olson of Minnesota, Warren Green of South Dakota, George Shafer of North Dakota, and Dan Turner of Iowa — met in Sioux City to hear farmers' complaints. Milo Reno told the governors that the Holiday Association, in addition to advocating holding actions, had three objectives: farm mortgage moratoriums, a special session of

Hollandale farm family which appealed for state help in 1929.

A MARCH FOR
SOCIAL JUSTICE & EQUALITY
Grant County Farmers Holiday
"AND WE DON'T MEAN MAYBE"

Congress to enact a farm credit bill, and state-enforced embargoes against the sale of farm products at less than production cost. The governors were sympathetic but could do little more than frame supportive resolutions.

The Minnesota Farmers' Holiday Association approached the farm problem in a less radical manner than did that of Iowa. Bosch understood that isolated farm strikes could not raise prices and that farmers could not reach even the cost of production without state and national legislation. Strikes, according to Bosch, would only draw attention to the farm problem, not solve it. When the Minnesota organization called for a thirty-day withholding action to begin on September 21, he warned the membership against picketing and violence. The strike had just begun, however, when farmers in the hard-hit counties of west-central Minnesota crowded onto the highways to protest farmers who were moving produce to market. In Yellow Medicine County an angry farmer shot and killed a twenty-five-year-old striker, the only casualty of the strike. Picketing was sporadic and short-lived, and on October 22 the strike ended. Governor Olson supported the non-violent farm strike and on October 11 issued a statement which told the public that the "farmers of Minnesota . . . have the right to join together in a so-called strike." Olson, like Bosch, recognized the significance of actions which called attention to the farm problem. He urged farmers to present a united front through organization. Speaking to a Farmers' Union convention in Montevideo in 1933, he confessed that he could not understand why farmers and workers had "laid down and taken it on the chin without a murmur." In his forceful style he proclaimed, "We need militarism in the farm movement."

The Minnesota Farmers' Holiday Association became the largest of all the state associations, and, in spite of New Deal measures to rescue agriculture, had 4,000 members in 1934. By 1936 its numbers dropped to just below 2,000, where it remained until its absorption by the Farmers' Union in late 1937. During 1936 and early 1937 President Bosch enthusiastically worked toward a union of all the radical farm movements, hoping for alliance with the newly formed Congress of Industrial Organizations. By mid-July 1937 he had made little progress and in disgust complained, "It is ten times easier to organize farmers against than for labor."

The Minnesota Farmers' Holiday Association focused attention on the farmer's precarious economic status. It succeeded in pressuring the 1933 legislature into passing a farm mortgage moratorium law and actively demonstrated in St. Paul when citizens' lobbies tried to coerce the legislature into remedial action. In spite of these accomplishments, the Minnesota Farmers' Holiday Association symbolized once again

Angry farmers march on the state capitol in 1933.

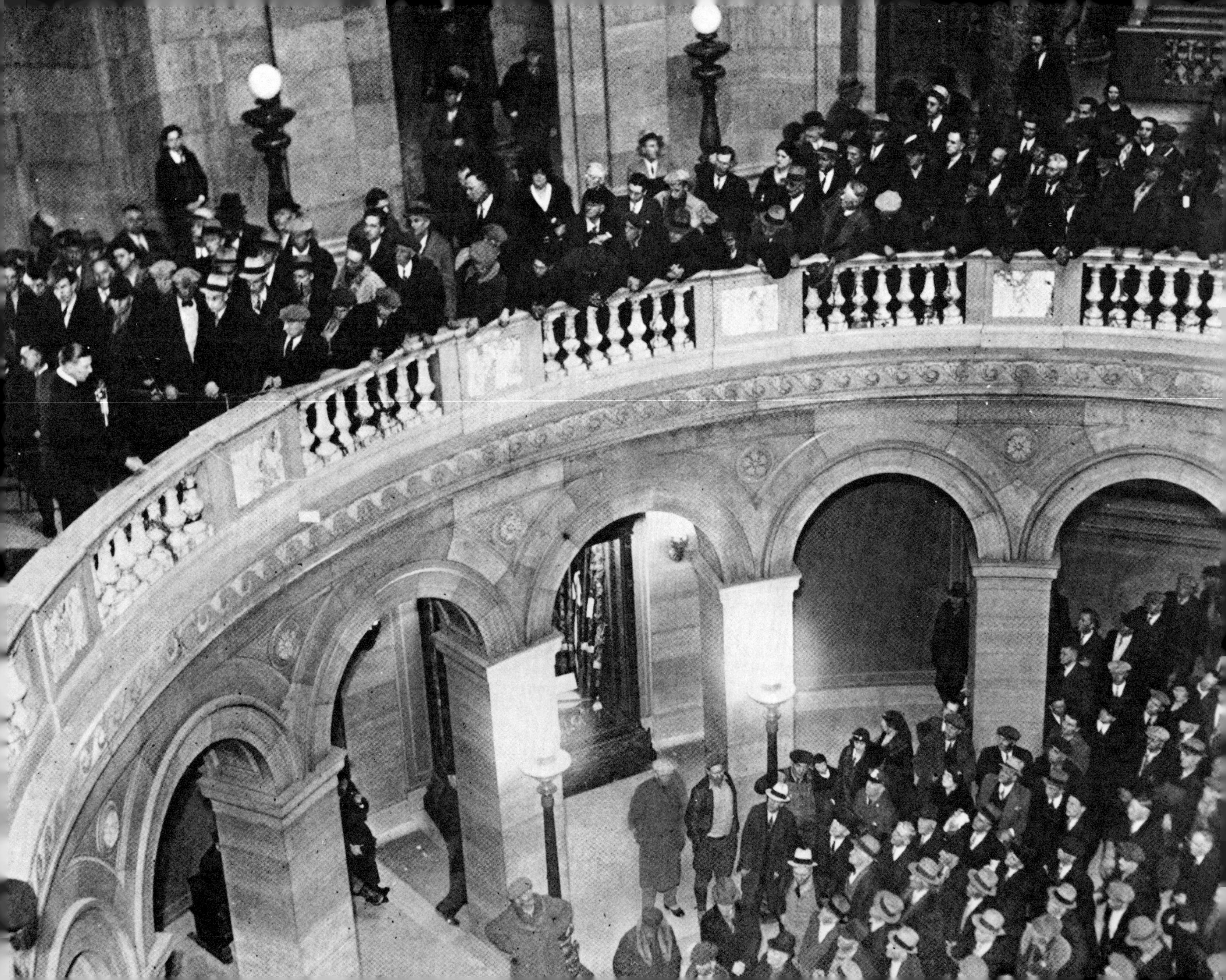

the inability of farmers to organize a cohesive and long-lasting united front.

The depression did not treat every farmer equally. The Goodhue or Houston county farmer weathered the storm much better than did the farmer who worked the land in Stevens or Big Stone counties. The number of people who depended upon federal relief during 1934 and 1935 reflects the general condition of Minnesota agriculture. If one excludes the thinly populated arrowhead counties of Cook and Lake, those counties in which 12 percent or less of the people received relief checks were clustered in southern Minnesota and the Red River Valley. Southern Minnesota fared better than any other area in the state. Many counties registered very low relief percentages: Faribault, 6; Houston, 6; Mower, 5; Nicollet, 5; Jackson, 5; Scott, 4; Wabasha, 4; Goodhue, 3.5. Southern Minnesota's low relief figures were due to several factors. Moisture was generally adequate to grow a crop and green the grass. Farms in the region were among the first settled; many had been in the same family for two generations, increasing the chances of lower debts. Farms were small, but diversified and more self-sufficient, producing hogs, poultry, cattle, dairy herds, corn, hay and mixed grains. The southern-Minnesota farmer had long ago abandoned his dependence upon one crop. The light industry and food-processing plants scattered throughout the rolling country further fortified the economy. This diversification played an instrumental role in the economic condition of the area.

The Red River Valley counties more nearly approached the 12 percent relief figure than did those in the south. Largely dependent upon wheat, those counties north from Wilkin salvaged reasonable crops due to rainfalls which were less than normal but adequate. Those counties in west-central Minnesota to the south of Wilkin were not spared the drought and grasshoppers which also ravaged the Dakotas. These wheat counties — where the Farmers' Holiday Association thrived — fell victim to the "Dakota drought," which wiped out hundreds of farmers in Big Stone, Stevens, Pope, and Swift counties. In Big Stone, the worst hit of Minnesota's counties, 60 percent of its residents struggled to survive on relief. Farmers to the east in counties such as Stearns, Kandiyohi, and Meeker fared a little better, not so much because of moisture, but because of diversification. The same was generally true of those counties in north-central Minnesota and those adjacent to the "12 percent or less" zone in the south.

Most Minnesota farmers, whether they were in the 12 or 60 percent relief areas, were in serious trouble. In a state where one-third of the population lived either on farms or in villages dependent on the farm dollar, the well-being of farmers was a critical factor in the health of the economy. Milo Reno may have oversimplified the impact of the restora-

Governor Floyd B. Olson (left with hand on rail) addresses the farmers in the capitol.

LEACH PROPOSES
TO SAVE
ONE-MILLION DOLLARS
for
CITIZENS ALLIANCE
by
STARVING 13,000
RELIEF CLIENTS
Join the WORKERS ALLIANCE
CAR STOP

tion of farm purchasing power, but it would have been impossible to persuade half of Minnesota's people that such would not "re-establish an endless chain of prosperity."

Three days after 2,000 farmers had selected John Bosch to lead their crusade against the depression, on August 1, 1932, almost 1,500 people crowded into the Methodist church in downtown Minneapolis not to attend a prayer meeting but to hear hard talk about economic survival. The minister of the church, George H. Mecklenburg, was deeply concerned about the plight of the people who lived in the neighborhood of his church; and he was determined to do something about it. "I couldn't go on preaching and see people hungry," he explained. "I had to do something." What the thoughtful clergyman did was to mastermind a unique device to combat the depression — the Organized Unemployed, Incorporated.

Mecklenburg firmly believed in the philosophy of self-help. To him, the outright government dole degraded the individual and led to moral decay, while work was spiritually uplifting. According to his scheme, the members of the Organized Unemployed would work on various projects and receive scrip at about 25 cents per hour for their labor; suppliers to the Organized Unemployed would also be paid in scrip. Thus, the scrip, which the organization printed, would become a medium of exchange. According to Mecklenburg, the members would become self-sufficient through the products which they made and the goods which they received in exchange.

The Mecklenburg movement to help those who would accept his motto, "Work not Dole," received wide support from Minneapolis businesses which supplied an initial $6,000 to help launch the effort; a restaurant owner provided complete cafeteria equipment. Farmers donated surplus crops; one gave 20,000 bushels of cabbage. The Board of Education let Mecklenburg use the old Central High School building, and soon it was a beehive of activity. The gift of cabbage turned the basement canning operation into a sauerkraut factory. The aroma of sauerkraut soon became a familiar trademark of the school's halls. A staff of 40 served 1,500 meals a day in the cafeteria; and others busied themselves at sewing machines, turning out clothing and bed linens. A scrip general store furnished members with goods which the Organized Unemployed itself did not make. In all operations barter was the means of conducting business. For example, the organization bartered sauerkraut for jacket material and then traded the finished jackets for a sugar processor. Not all activities centered in the high school. During 1933 Mecklenburg placed about 100 families on abandoned farms. The families gained a living, and the Organized Unemployed received surplus commodities. Several crews of members cut wood, providing still another item for the membership and for exchange.

Unemployed workers picket the Minneapolis city hall in 1937.

ORGANIZE
STRIKE
AGAINST
LOW WAGES
VOTE COMMUNIST
We Demand
WORK
WAGES
FIGHT
UNEMPLOYMENT
INSURANCE
FUND
COMMUNIST
CANDIDATES
JOIN!
COMMUNIST
PARTY
We Demand
WORK
WAGES

During the first year over $60,000 in scrip went into circulation. Many Minneapolis businesses, as well as professional people, accepted the scrip for goods and services. Mecklenburg claimed that over 8,000 unemployed had been aided during the first year of operation, and he began to talk about organizing all the unemployed in Minnesota. In spite of this optimism, the Organized Unemployed faced an uncertain future. It could neither produce nor provide enough variety of goods to become self-sufficient, and it lacked funds to obtain them. When the New Deal began the Federal Emergency Relief Administration, Mecklenburg's group received $20,000 from the Division of Self-Help Cooperatives, providing capital to continue into 1934. The infusion of federal money, however, robbed the Organized Unemployed of its unique self-help concept. Soon it became a part of the vast state relief network and during 1935 came to an end. Yet Mecklenburg's dream had saved thousands of people in a desperate hour. In those days before federal funds entered the fight against depression, the Organized Unemployed, Incorporated, had given downtrodden city people a spark of hope, just as the Holiday Association had for farmers.

Although Minnesotans tried to solve their own problems, the depression was a nationwide phenomenon beyond the scope of their local control. The Minnesota Farmers' Holiday Association could not push up farm prices. The Organized Unemployed could not employ all the jobless in the Twin Cities. Minnesota's state government could not deal with bank failures, unemployment, or farm prices. An acute national problem had to be attacked by the federal government, and that is what Franklin D. Roosevelt pledged to do as he took office in March 1933. The President promised the people a New Deal, and he and Congress acted swiftly to counter the effect of the depression.

In June 1933 Congress responded to the farm crisis and passed the Agricultural Adjustment Act — one of the first pieces of major New Deal legislation. The act established the Agricultural Adjustment Administration (AAA), which had the responsibility for raising farm prices by restricting the supply of commodities. Although the program depended upon the voluntary cooperation of farmers, AAA controlled the "acreage allotment." It would determine a total acreage of crops to be planted in the next growing season and allocate allotments to each farm on the basis of that farm's recent crop history. In return for cutting production, the farmer received a "benefit check." For example, wheat farmers received about 30 cents a bushel on 54 percent of their average production. AAA financed the benefit payments through a food-processing tax levied on millers and meatpackers. In 1936 the Supreme Court ruled the processing tax to be invalid, and the AAA scheme abruptly ended. Immediately Congress passed the

Communists rally in St. Paul, 1930.

Soil Conservation and Domestic Allotment Act, which empowered the Secretary of Agriculture to make contracts with and pay benefits to farmers who would reduce the acreage of soil-depleting crops and rebuild the land. Because crop production rose in 1937, Congress enacted a new Agricultural Adjustment Act which maintained the soil-conservation basis of acreage allotment but reinforced the principle of direct support to prices. All three acts were designed to provide the farmer with "equality" or "parity" to bring farm prices more in line with the prices the farmer had to pay for goods.

Headlines across the state hailed the advent of AAA checks. A Polk County newspaper greeted the payments with "MILLIONS INTO MINNESOTA." To the south in Big Stone County the checks were heralded with "GOVERNMENT FUNDS SAVE FARMERS." "The difference between 1932 and 1935," observed a Nobles County extension agent, "was the difference between night and day, and part of it was due to . . . farm programs."

The Roosevelt administration proposed the Federal Emergency Relief Act (FERA) to furnish immediate help to relieve rural and urban hardship. To inaugurate the program, Congress appropriated $500,000,000. Although the legislation called for states to match federal money (one state dollar for three federal), states which could not match were not penalized. Under FERA the federal government made direct grants to the office of the governor, and it became the governor's responsibility to establish a state system of administration. Since relief historically had been a function of states and local groups, this technique provided the most rapid means of alleviating the physical sufferings of the people.

During the period of FERA (1933-1935) Minnesotans received $67,619,854 for work relief, direct relief, emergency education, and college-student aid. State and county matching funds totaled over $13,500,000. When FERA began in July 1933 only a little over six percent of Minnesota's population went on relief. With each passing day more people applied for federal aid, and by December 1934 over 18 percent had enrolled in the program — a much lower percentage than that of the drought-stricken Dakotas but higher then either Wisconsin or Iowa.

FERA not only provided cash relief but also encouraged work projects which touched most places in Minnesota. With over a half million people in the program, few communities did not benefit from school renovation, road improvement, or the building of recreational facilities such as baseball diamonds, tennis courts, golf courses, playgrounds, swimming pools, and skating rinks. Not all FERA projects dealt with construction. FERA teachers kept open almost 200 schools; hot lunch and smallpox

Federal project workers lay sidewalks in Fergus Falls.

immunization programs served thousands of children. FERA's surplus relief program distributed beef, veal, pork, cereals, and fruit to the needy. Sewing projects turned surplus cotton into clothing, sheets, and towels. To those who faced starvation, the surplus commodities program meant the difference between life and death. The program supplied Minnesotans with over $5,000,000 worth of cloth goods and farm produce. Compared to North Dakota ($8,000,000) and South Dakota ($8,700,000), the Minnesota share is low per capita, but high in comparison with Iowa ($1,400,000) and Wisconsin ($3,300,000). In all, FERA pumped almost $75,000,000 into the Minnesota economy, directly serving one in every five Minnesotans. It provided the state with better roads, more recreational facilities, and improved school buildings; but more significantly it lifted the spirits of the people.

In November 1933 the President, under authority which the National Industrial Recovery Act gave him, established the Civil Works Program to complement FERA. Intended to put money into the economy within a short period of time between November 1933 and July 1934, the Civil Works Administration (CWA) injected almost a billion dollars into the economy. By January 1934 CWA had employed over four million men. Although the federal government administered the program, state and local boards planned and supervised the projects. Minnesota received $19,608,000 in CWA funds. The Minnesota program employed almost 200,000 people in a variety of work projects, most of which were similar to those of FERA. People who were not suited for manual labor received employment in the Civil Works Service section of the Civil Works Program. Drafting construction plans, surveying roads, working at weather bureaus and libraries, and sewing were included in the activities of the CWS.

In 1935 FERA came to an end, and in its place the New Deal set up the Works Progress Administration (WPA). Under the new system state and local government once again became responsible for out-right monetary relief, and the federal government directed all work relief. WPA carried on the same kinds of work projects which had been done under FERA; it did, however, tackle larger projects such as bridges and public buildings. WPA emphasized the best use of those whose talents went beyond the shovel. For example, the WPA Federal Writers Project prepared an excellent guide on Minnesota. At the historical society WPA workers compiled an index of Minnesotans who had served in the military during the Civil War and a bibliography of Minnesota's weekly newspapers from 1925 to 1941. Painters taught community art classes, and musicians played in federal bands. Every county in the state enjoyed both the employment and the enrichment which WPA furnished.

Federal project workers on a Rochester sewing project.

During its first month of operation 54,000 Minnesotans took advantage of the new work relief program. WPA enrollment reached its peak in 1938 with an average of 60,600 Minnesotans employed each month by the program. Per capita federal expenditures for WPA earnings ranged between $15.00 and $17.49 per month. In no month did WPA employ more than three percent of Minnesota's total population, but estimates place the number of those helped, including dependent children, as high as a half million Minnesotans. The number of people employed by WPA in Minnesota was very close to the national average. With 100 representing the national WPA employment rate, Minnesota stood at 101, much higher than Iowa, 54, much lower than North Dakota, 174, and South Dakota, 199, and about the same as Wisconsin, 99.

Two New Deal depression programs, the Civilian Conservation Corps (CCC) and the National Youth Administration (NYA), were designed for the young. In April 1933 the CCC began operation to furnish work and training to young men who were unemployed and to carry out a nation-wide conservation program. Like most New Deal programs CCC was more than just relief; it had a broader purpose. CCC enrollees improved forests and parks, helped control soil erosion, developed recreational areas, worked on flood control projects, and assisted in the protection of wild life. For example, the Indian Division of CCC sponsored several worthwhile projects on Minnesota reservations. At Rice Lake on the White Earth Reservation a crew of 35 Chippewa developed ricing camps and improved accessibility to the rice areas. At Nett Lake 200 labored to build Corp facilities from which to launch other projects. Through the years 2,500,000 found such employment in the CCC. In Minnesota men from every county participated in the program, which employed an average of about 13,000 each month. Each worker earned $30.00 a month, of which $25.00 was sent home to his family. A majority of non-urban Native Americans received help from CCC, improving somewhat their gloomy living conditions.

The National Youth Administration (NYA), administered by WPA, provided part-time employment for students between the ages of 16 and 24. High school students could earn $6.00 per month, college students up to $20.00, and graduate students up to $30.00. Most students did light construction work, research, or library work. CCC and NYA gave young people renewed confidence in the system and, at the same time, injected about $400,000 into the Minnesota economy during peak months.

AAA provided more economic security for farmers. FERA brought immediate help to both farmers and laborers. WPA gave work to many of the cities' jobless. Labor's greatest boom during the 1930s, however, was the passage of the National Industrial Recovery

WPA weed-cutting project in St. Paul.

Act (NIRA) of 1933, a partnership of business, labor and government, which gave employees the right to organize and to bargain collectively. Under the law, an employer could not force workers to join a company union nor interfere with their efforts to organize a union of their own. The act gave the labor movement new vitality.

The business prosperity of the 1920s had lulled workers into organizational inactivity. Many lost interest in the labor movement because of high employment and good wages. The American Federation of Labor (AFL), for example, lost over 600,000 members; and the development of new unions faltered. The onset of the depression after 1929 and the ensuing mass unemployment bewildered both labor leadership and the rank and file workers. Between 1929 and 1933 the AFL lost almost a half million members, dropping its numbers to 2,300,000. Other unions experienced similar declines. Neither the workers nor union leadership knew how to cope with the chaos which total depression had created.

Under the New Deal the established and generally accepted unions such as the AFL once again flourished. By the end of 1936 the AFL had gained over 700,000 members. Labor leaders vigorously seized upon the guarantee of collective bargaining and the plight of workers to organize new locals and recruit new members. NIRA was intended to create harmony between labor and management. In Minnesota it brought strike and bloodshed.

Minnesota traditionally had not been fertile ground for labor organizers. Minneapolis' reputation as an anti-union city was widespread because the Citizens' Alliance, an organization of businessmen formed in 1908, had effectively kept organized labor weak. Although pledged to improve working conditions and the promotion of harmony between management and labor, the Alliance supported anti-union politicians and hired informants to infiltrate labor's ranks. The Minnesota worker, however, had an advantage that his counterpart in other states did not have: a political party in power which was pledged to improve the position of labor. The Farmer-Labor party's first test came in November 1933, when a dispute between workers and the Hormel Company threatened to tear apart the city of Austin.

Disgruntled with declining wages and owner Jay Hormel's "benevolent absolutism," workers at the Austin meat processing plant became extremely disenchanted when Hormel tried to force them to participate in a retirement program which would have resulted in a weekly twenty-cent reduction in pay. On the evening of July 13 the Hormel workers gathered in a park to discuss their grievances against the company. Unionization seemed to be the only solution to the problem, and on the following day Frank Ellis, a

The 1934 Minneapolis drivers' strike: violence begins.

Hormel employee with years of union experience, engineered the formation of a local union, the Independent Union of All Workers which would be open to all workers in the area.

During fall of 1933 the new union decided that the time was ripe to press for a collective bargaining agreement with Hormel, even if it meant a strike. The threat of a strike forced Hormel to recognize the union in an agreement which would give the union two of its important demands: a seniority system and arbitration of grievances. In early November the Independent Union asked for a twenty-cent hourly wage increase, and when Hormel refused, the leadership of the Union called a strike. Workers tossed management out of the plant and took it over; Hormel began to look for two-hundred strike-breakers; sheriff's deputies tried to keep order; the people of Austin feared that strife would soon be upon their community.

The sheriff sent out a plea to Governor Olson for intervention: "Situation here so unruly that deputizing of un-uniformed and poorly armed citizens would precipitate guerilla warfare with pitiful casualties on both sides . . . I appeal to you to dispatch militia to take situation before nightfall at the latest." Olson did not reply but secretly stationed three hundred national guardsmen at nearby Owatonna. When the situation deteriorated, Olson personally went to Austin to intervene. He forced Hormel to agree to arbitration of the dispute by the state's Industrial Commission. The Commission granted pay increases of between two and four cents per hour and a formal grievance procedure. Even though it was disappointed over the low wage settlement, the Independent Union claimed victory.

When two Twin City newspapers objected to what they considered to be Olson's pro-labor handling of the strike, the Governor went on WCCO radio to defend his position. He assured his listeners that Hormel "expressed complete satisfaction with the manner in which the situation had been handled." Pledging never to use his office to break a strike, he sarcastically apologized to what he termed "the reactionary press" because he "did not turn the machine guns of the state upon some 2700 citizens of the state and create some widows and orphans." He lashed out against the "Keepers of the Sacred Cow of Property" in words that encouraged workers in their drive for better conditions:

> *These blood-thirsty swivel-chair warriors whose only knowledge of life is gained through travelling from their homes to the sanctuary of their editorial rooms, thence to their exclusive clubs, and then back home, having no knowledge of the reactions of working people's affairs nor of their pride; their aspirations; their*

The 1934 Minneapolis drivers' strike: strikers vs. strike breakers.

> *ideals; their ambitions — are undertaking to state in substance that men should not be reasoned with, but should be struck down and killed . . . They do not know that it needs but a spark to start a veritable conflagration in this Nation, and in their supreme egotism I presume they do not care.*

Olson's position seemed clear. He was the workers' governor.

When in 1933 and 1934 labor organizers singled out Minneapolis truckers as a target for activity, the Citizens' Alliance became outraged. Outrage turned to violent opposition when Daniel Tobin, head of the International Teamsters' Union, selected Carl Skoglund and Vince Dunne, along with Dunne's two brothers, to spearhead the drive to unionize all truckers in the city. The four were tough, skilled organizers who were dedicated to the triumph of the working class.

The first union effort to demonstrate muscle came during the cold month of February 1934, when coal companies would not meet with truck drivers who were represented by Local 574. Dunne and Skoglund ordered a walk-out on February 7, and 700 workers left their jobs. Unprepared for such bold and decisive action, the companies agreed to recognize the union and to start salary talks, ending the walk out. The initial success of Local 574 generated 2,000 new members within a month.

In late April, Local 574 declared its objectives: a closed shop, shorter hours, a $27.50 per week average wage, and overtime pay. The Citizens' Alliance scurried into an emergency session at which it set up the Employers' Committee to negotiate with the workers. Throughout the first two weeks of May nothing was accomplished. In spite of the union's withdrawal of its closed shop demand and the intervention of the Regional Labor Board, the Employers' Committee stalled; the drivers threatened to strike.

Believing that the public had rallied to its side, the union, admittedly gambling with its future, voted to strike on May 16. Both sides looked to Governor Olson for support. Because he was labor's governor and had championed the rights of the working man, the union expected him to force management to its knees. The Citizens' Alliance, in contrast, thought he would break the strike to protect the well-being of the public and to acknowledge the political support many businessmen had given him during the 1930 and 1932 elections. In charting his course of action, however, Governor Olson attempted to stay on neutral ground.

The Citizens' Alliance and Local 574 prepared for a long struggle. The Alliance hired 400 strike breakers; the union armed its people with clubs; city police readied themselves; Olson threatened martial law. The tension soon erupted into bloody violence. Several hundred union pickets marched into the market area. Expecting a union demonstration,

The 1934 Minneapolis drivers' strike: police move in.

the Citizens' Alliance "army" was waiting. The sight of the determined strikers quickly scattered the "army"; police, however, attempted to halt the advance of the strikers. The fracas left three dozen people injured.

This was only a dress rehearsal. The next day thousands returned to the market: strikers, the Citizens' Alliance "army," police, curious on lookers, and personnel from a St. Paul radio station to cover the spectacle. Within seconds after someone had smashed a window, the sound of gunfire, clubs cracking skulls, shouts of anger, and cries of pain echoed throughout the market. After an hour's battle, two members of the citizens' "army" lay dead on the blood-spattered pavement.

With the National Guard ready for action and with pressure from the Governor and the National Labor Relations Board, the opposing sides put down their weapons and began once again to talk. Olson and the other mediators worked feverishly to settle the impasse and on May 26 convinced both sides to accept a compromise and end the strike. Soon, however, the union began complaining that management was not keeping the bargain: wages began to decline and hours increased; many strikers had not been rehired. During June the disagreement flared into a name-calling campaign to gain public sympathy. The Citizens' Alliance claimed that the union was little more than a communist offensive; through its new publication, *The Organizer,* Local 574 waged a relentless attack on the dishonesty and trickery of Minneapolis businessmen. By early July the deteriorating situation had become a conflict between "communism" and "capitalism."

The union demanded that negotiations reopen; when the Employers' Committee did not budge Local 574, now 7,000 strong, again struck on July 16. Fearing the worst, Police Chief Mike Johannes outfitted an additional 800 men with shotguns, bayonets, and clubs. Governor Olson refused to assign the National Guard to duty but did place one unit at the Minneapolis armory. On July 20 a clash between strikers and police resulted in the wounding of 67 and the killing of two. Intensified hostilities placed Minneapolis on the verge of class warfare. When an Olson compromise failed, due largely to the opposition of the Citizens' Alliance, an angry Governor declared martial law. No liquor could be sold after 9 p.m., and streets had to be cleared by midnight. Strikers could not picket, and trucks could not move without a permit. Union leaders accused Olson of trying to break the strike; employers blamed him for not breaking the strike. On July 30 the Governor explained role of the Guard in the strike. "The National Guard is not here to take orders from them [employers]," he explained, "nor is it here primarily to aid them in the operations of their businesses. Neither is it here to help the union. It is here in the interests of the rest of the people of the city, who totally outnumber the members of both contend-

The 1934 Minneapolis drivers' strike: police restore order.

ing forces." His sympathy for the workers' side became apparent, however, when he attacked Twin Cities' newspapers for favoring the large advertisers in their strike stories. "The grimy workingman who sweats long hours for $12.00 a week cannot advertise," the Governor complained.

The strike dragged on until August 21. Then, a settlement was unexpectedly announced: a minimum wage of 50 cents per hour for drivers and re-employment of strikers, and recognition of the union. It is likely that this surprising conclusion came as a result of a threat from the White House to withhold essential government loans from businesses in Minneapolis unless the strike ended. After four months, hundreds of injuries, and four deaths, the long and violent strike was over.

In early June 1935 labor lost its guarantees concerning organization and bargaining when the United State Supreme Court declared the National Industrial Recovery Act to be unconstitutional. The Citizens' Alliance leaped at the opportunity to spurn labor's requests for negotiations. A Minneapolis ornamental iron works company abruptly halted talks with its workers, and they struck in early July. Police and pickets scuffled often while the company operated the plant with non-union people. Only after stray police fire killed two onlookers did the plant close, and by mid-September the company finally yielded to the demands for official recognition and salary increases. By that time Senator Robert Wagner of New York had succeeded in salvaging labor's rights through the National Labor Relations Act, which renewed the guarantee of recognition and collective bargaining. The National Labor Relations Act, however, had no impact on Mrs. J.H. Struthers, president of Strutwear Knitting Mills. Through late summer, fall, winter, and early spring of 1935-1936 she steadfastly fought the Hosiery Workers Union. In spite of court action and brutal confrontations, in April 1936 the company, facing financial problems, recognized the union and negotiated a satisfactory wage increase. Eight months of company resistance had failed.

Turbulence in labor-management relations continued into the administration of Governor Elmer Benson. Olson's sympathies had always been on the side of workingmen, but he tempered that support because of his need for votes from conservatives. Many times labor was disappointed with the Farmer-Labor governor; only when circumstances forced him did he seem to come out fighting for workers in strike situations. Governor Benson, in contrast, was direct, said what he thought, and did not worry about offending businessmen. One banker is alleged to have said that the difference between Olson and Benson was that, while both spoke the same language, Benson believed in it.

The 1934 Minneapolis drivers' strike: death and injury.

1039

Benson had been in office only a few days when lumberjacks, newly affiliated with the Timber and Sawmill Workers, went on strike, closing down northern Minnesota's vast lumber operations. The powerful Weyerhauser interests refused to recognize the new local union and had no intention of submitting to labor's demands. The Governor acted immediately to protect the striking lumberjacks from the bitter cold of January 1937. He provided the strikers with food and shelter through the state's relief agencies, brought in the highway patrol to keep peace, and ordered a citizens' investigation into working conditions at the lumber camps. Within a few days, the lumberjacks had a contract which recognized the union and provided an 18 percent wage increase. A few weeks later, when a strike of electrical workers against Northern States Power Company threatened Minneapolis with a termination of power, Benson hinted that he would use the National Guard to run the plants if a settlement were not soon reached. A few hours later the company and the union signed a new contract.

In late May the American Gas Machine Company at Albert Lea fired several of its employees for promoting the Independent Union of All Workers. When the company adamantly refused to rehire the workers, the union staged a peaceful sit-down strike in protest. Only when the company obtained an injunction did the workers leave to set up picket lines outside the building. Agitation over the union spread into the community, where a citizens' committee promised to stamp out unionism. The sheriff, who had deputized a "small army" of men, gave the committee his support and drilled his men, armed with shotguns, in the town's auditorium. Tension mounted as dozens of union sympathizers from other cities converged on Albert Lea to support their fellow unionists. Afraid of a union rebellion, the sheriff jailed several union leaders. Certain that the sheriff and citizens' committee would unleash an all-out assault on the workers, the union called a mass meeting for April 1 at which it planned to explain its position to the town's residents. The sheriff, however, refused to wait for the meeting and took control of the plan arresting the union pickets. Moving to union headquarters, the sheriff's men rousted out the members with tear gas and marched them off to jail. Angered by these strong-arm tactics, hundreds of workers from Austin, Minneapolis, St. Paul, and Duluth poured into Albert Lea. Within hours 2,000 unionists swarmed through the streets, taking control of the American Gas Machine plant and driving the sheriff and his men behind barricades in the jail. Albert Lea was on the verge of civil war.

Rioting during the American Gas Machine Company strike in Albert Lea, 1937.

Unable to cope with the situation, the mayor called Governor Benson, urging him to come personally to resolve the conflict on April 2. That afternoon Benson's automobile pulled into Albert Lea. The Governor ordered the sheriff to release the union members,

scolded the company for violations of the National Labor Relations Act, and forced it to the bargaining table. After a night of tough bargaining, the company gave in and extended recognition to the Independent Union of All Workers. The Governor's intercession had spared Albert Lea from a labor war.

Labor's struggle in Minnesota during the 1930s ended on a strange, stormy, and tragic note. During the hot days of early July 1939, WPA workers went on strike. Congress had just reduced their hourly wage and had increased the work week. WPA workers who had been employed for a continuous 18 months' period would be laid off. Because Congress had acted at the last hour, most workers did not find out about the change until they reported for work after the July Fourth holiday. When they discovered that they would have to work more hours for less pay, in many cases for half pay, they rebelled. Upset over what they considered to be dishonest and cavalier treatment, 18,000 workers, 10,000 in Minneapolis, walked off their projects. WPA officials threatened to fire workers, and within a few days most projects closed. Road graders stood still on unfinished roads; sidewalks remained uncompleted, the Minneapolis Federal Symphony Band played without its drum section.

Organized labor immediately gave its support to the WPA strikers and urged officials to close down all projects until the dispute had been settled. The WPA took a hard line and announced that those who did not return to their projects by July 10 would be fired. When police escorted nonstriking workers through picket lines, trouble began. Although anyone who attempted to keep non-strikers from working was subject to felony charges, strikers became angry and on July 10 clashed with police at a sewing project; one policeman died of a heart attack. Daily scuffles with police prompted WPA officials to demand additional protection for the non-strikers. The day began uneventfully, but more and more strikers began to drift toward the project as the day wore on. That evening when the 200 non-strikers began to leave, tempers flared. The police resorted to tear gas and, in the heat of the moment, opened fire to disperse the crowd. When order had been restored, seventeen people had been injured and an elderly worker had been shot to death. Mayor George Leach warned that he would no longer allow his police to protect non-strikers. WPA officials had little choice but to close down all projects and to work toward a settlement. A committee of strikers met with WPA officials in the office of the state's new Republican governor, Harold Stassen, and by July 21 had hammered out a compromise which ended the strike.

Aftermath of the rioting at the American Gas Machine Company, Albert Lea, 1937.

Although WPA workers had struck in several cities, the government singled out Minneapolis for a federal investigation. Two days after the settlement, a federal grand

jury convened in St. Paul to determine whether or not WPA strikers had violated the law. The investigation revealed that 25 FBI agents, disguised as workers, had infiltrated the WPA ranks of strikers. The grand jury plodded on for three weeks and on August 18 indicted 162 workers, most of whom were charged with interfering with workers who did not strike — a felony. In some cases conspiracy charges were added to the indictments. Federal District Judge Robert Bell set bail at an average of $5,000 per person. Since the entire WPA force collectively could not have raised bail for just one person, the Central Labor Union, in a display of labor cooperation, began to work for reduction in bail. Only after three weeks of negotiations and after putting up the labor temple as security did the union succeed in freeing the WPA strikers.

On October 3 the trials began. The strikers were tried not as individuals but as groups (according to the incident and charges involved). After three trials, the proceedings ended in mid-November. Thirty-two workers were convicted; of these, 15 went to jail for periods ranging from 30 days to eight months, and 17 received suspended sentences. No further trials were held and the remaining cases, about 120, were dismissed. Why Minneapolis was selected as a target for federal investigation is not entirely clear. The federal government — perhaps the President himself — wanted to demonstrate that it did not take the WPA strikes lightly and Minneapolis may have been chosen because of communist activity within the unions.

Whether one worked in an Austin packing plant, in the forests near Duluth, in a Minneapolis truck, in the iron-ore pits near Hibbing, or in a St. Paul factory, the decade of the 1930s was one of hardship and struggle. Yet, in spite of the death and injury, the chaos and turmoil, labor emerged from the 1930s politically and economically stronger than before. By the end of the decade even the staunchest opponents of organized labor began to recognize that unions had become a fact of life. The New Deal had given workers legislation with which to gain more security.

Just as the depression did not treat farmers and workers alike, it did not affect all businesses similarly. Well-managed and conservatively run enterprises withstood the test of economic trouble; others faltered. Just a few days after the stock market crash of October 1929, the highly-speculative business empire of Wilbur B. Foshay collapsed. Only two months earlier 32-story Foshay Tower, a Minneapolis skyscraper, had been dedicated. John Philip Sousa had directed his band in the stirring "Foshay Tower March" as 20,000 people witnessed the dedication of the multi-million-dollar building. Foshay had pulled together a business operation which held utility companies, banks, hotels, mills and factories, and retail stores in Minnesota, eleven other states, Canada, Mexico,

Police disperse pickets with tear gas during the strike against the **Duluth News Tribune,** *1938.*

Y
544
9

and Central America. Heavily invested in the stockmarket, Foshay could not withstand the crash and his empire crumbled.

Financially sound and conservatively administered businesses such as General Mills, Minneapolis-Honeywell, and Dayton's weathered the depression. General Mills showed a steady increase in net income during the 1930s — even through the dark years of 1931, 1932, and 1933. Minneapolis-Honeywell showed a precipitous decline in revenues in 1931 and 1932 and cut its numbers of employees nearly by half. Due to the production of new items — such as flour sifters for the Pillsbury Company — income recovered in 1933 and the company's employment returned to normal. In 1934 it bought out the Brown Instrument Company of Philadelphia, and by the end of 1936 its sales and employees more than tripled. George Draper Dayton's downtown department store in Minneapolis made a profit each year of the depression through innovative promotion. Using sales gimmicks such as anniversary sales and special discount days, the store established a model which many others imitated to keep people buying.

Banking, so central to the well-being of the business community, reflected a similar pattern. Weak banks fell early to economic contraction. In 1921 Minnesota had 1,506 banks; by 1930, 491 had closed their doors, leaving 1,015 in operation. In 1931 alone, 93 state and national banks folded. State Auditor Ray P. Chase observed that "too many banks have been probably the largest single cause of bank failures." The situation which existed in St. Peter, a town of 4,335 people, supported Chase's reasoning. Three banks in that small, Minnesota Valley community vied for business during the early 1920s. The national average was one bank for each 3,500 people; St. Peter had too many banks; and in 1924 its Citizens Bank closed. Like St. Peter's Citizens Bank, many Minnesota banks were overextended and had loaned heavily in western farm land; and when hard times struck the farms after 1921, the banks were caught in a money-flow bind. In contrast, First National Bank of St. Peter, with conservative management, weathered the depression. By 1933 its assets had declined 22 percent, and its losses on farm paper and in bond accounts were higher than profits, forcing the use of undivided profits and surplus funds. Yet St. Peter's First National Bank survived.

The formation in Minnesota of two large bank-holding companies strengthened the state's economy. In early 1929 the Northwest Bank Corporation and the First Bank Stock Corporation began business. Organized to bolster the Ninth Federal Revenue District's sagging bank system, the two holding companies grew rapidly. For example, within a year the Northwest Bank Corporation had acquired 90 banks and by 1931 had controlling interest in 127 banks. Both companies funnelled money into troubled banks, giving more

Funeral of Emil Bergstrom, victim of the WPA strike.

stability to Minnesota's banking network. The New Deal's Bank Holiday and ensuing remedial legislation such as insured deposits gave banks a firmer foundation upon which to operate and increased public confidence in the banking and business system.

The depression touched all Minnesotans. During the bleak days of 1932 and 1933 the people were filled with anxiety and fear; they seemed to be in an uncontrollable situation. Somehow their world was collapsing around them, and they were bewildered. Without the intervention of the federal government, Minnesotans could not have survived the terrible Thirties. The farmer, the laborer, the businessman, and the banker depended on New Deal programs to relieve the hardship and to reform the system. The $1,080,000,960 which the New Deal pumped into Minnesota between 1933 and 1939 gave people work, stabilized the economy, lifted spirits, and allayed fears. Citizens grumbled occasionally about the massive bureaucracy which had enveloped them, but most of them realized that that was the price of survival.

"Happy days are here again." WPA day camp at St. Cloud.

II. "JUST BEYOND THE HORIZON IS RAMPANT LAWLESSNESS": POLITICAL TURMOIL

"Capitalism as we know it is doomed," declared Governor Elmer Benson in 1936. "I am convinced that nothing short of social ownership of key industries can save us." For a state which had remained within the mainstream of American politics since entering the Union in 1858, those were radical words — words which reflected the agony and the frustration of the depression years.

Although Minnesotans had elected two Populists to Congress in the 1890s, they rejected Populism in state-wide elections and remained faithful to the Republican party. The Progressive mood of reform which swept the nation during the years before World War I touched Minnesota, but Minnesotans were cautious and did not embrace reforms such as the initiative and referendum which gave direct political power to the people. During World War I, Minnesotans did not allow the Nonpartisan League and its program of state ownership to spill over from neighboring North Dakota. At the same time the

COLFAX 5596
KEYS

Minnesota legislature established the Minnesota Commission of Public Safety, an ultra-conservative state agency which was created to safeguard Minnesotans from activities which were not consistent with the Constitution and to promote "true American ideals." The rejection of the League and the acceptance of the Commission symbolized the state's conservative nature; Minnesota was not fertile ground for political change.

During the 1920s Minnesota remained in conservative hands under Republican governors J.A.O. Preus (1921-1925), Theodore Christianson (1925-1931), and Republican-controlled legislatures. But a growing coalition of farmers and workers challenged that power and forced the Republicans into concessions such as the rural-credit plan and taxes on iron ore. In 1922 farmer-labor coalition entered a full slate of third-party candidates in the fall general election and shocked the Republicans and Democrats by electing two United States representatives and a senator. The election of Henrick Shipstead, a Glenwood dentist, to the Senate demonstrated that farmer-labor cooperation could bring success in a state-wide election; cooperative political effort seemed to be the only answer.

In 1924 the Farmer-Labor Federation, which represented the Minnesota Farmers' Nonpartisan league and the Working People's Nonpartisan Political League, backed a political newcomer for Governor — Floyd B. Olson, the relatively obscure state's attorney of Hennepin County. Olson's opponents hammered away at the radical nature of the Federation and constantly reminded the voters that the Federation-endorsed candidate had the support of communists. Olson lost to Theodore Christianson by 40,000 votes, but the Federation learned two valuable lessons: the danger of flaunting radicalism and the need for establishing a grass-roots organization. After the election the Farmer-Labor Federation dissolved, and the Farmer-Labor Association replaced it. This new political faction had as its main objective the union of all farmers and laborers for the promotion of their own economic interests. The Association called for an end to monopoly and proposed a system of state-ownership. It banned communists from membership in an attempt to rid itself of the aura of radicalism. To entrench itself as a permanent political force, the Association promoted the formation of farmer-labor clubs at the local level, which a statewide executive committee would coordinate, and called for the endorsement of candidates in local elections. Although the Association succeeded in electing some candidates in local contests, in 1926 and 1928 Christianson easily defeated its gubernatorial candidates.

Martial law, Minneapolis, 1934.

Midway through Christianson's third term, the stockmarket crashed; by election time of 1930, depression began to cast its long shadow across the land. Even before the

KSTP

crash Floyd B. Olson was confident that farmer-labor combine had become strong enough for him to risk another run for the governorship. As the successful Hennepin state's attorney, he had gained the respect of a broad spectrum of Twin Cities people — even bankers and Republicans. Across the state he was the best known and most probable candidate whom the farmer-laborites could put forward. Although the full fury of the depression had not struck by November 1930, the deteriorating economic conditions certainly would work to the advantage of the out-party.

Olson waged a skillful and deliberate campaign. Remembering the fiasco of 1924, he selected his words carefully and followed a middle-ground position. Although the voting public knew that the farmer-laborites stood for a system of state-ownership, listening to Olson gave his party little inkling that he was indeed their candidate. Realizing that he needed votes from Republicans and Democrats and taking advantage of internal squabbles in both parties, Olson presented himself as the candidate of all the people. His eloquence, enhanced by an imposing stage presence, struck out against injustice and governmental mismanagement — but in terms which frightened none. Republican candidate Ray P. Chase, the well-liked and youthful state auditor, had great difficulty finding fault with Olson; and Democrat Edward Indrehus barely tried to. The strength of his personality, the weakness of the opposition, and the economic situation brought Olson a smashing victory at the polls: Olson, 473,154; Chase, 289,528; Indrehus, 29,109. This was a personal victory; Olson's landslide carried only one farmer-labor candidate into state office and failed even to give his followers many seats in the "nonpartisan" legislature.

The thirty-nine year old Olson brought both youth and compassion to the office. He had grown up in a poor Norwegian-Swedish home located in an impoverished Jewish neighborhood on Minneapolis' northside. His family had little money, so as a boy Olson worked at odd jobs around the city. After graduation from high school and a year at the University of Minnesota, he traveled west, taking what jobs were available: grain harvesting, mining, fishing, and dock working. In 1913 he returned to Minneapolis, where he became a clerk in a law office and entered Northwestern Law College. After admission to the bar in 1915, Olson joined the firm of Larabee and Davies. During the war years he remained a Democrat and in 1918 and 1920 unsuccessfully tried to get a nomination for Congress. In 1919 he was appointed assistant state's attorney and in 1920 was named state's attorney to fill out an unexpired term. He earned a reputation as a capable prosecutor — a reputation which won him election several times to that post. His boy-

Governor Floyd B. Olson addresses Minnesotans during his inauguration.

RARIG'S KID DOESN'T STARVE WHY SHOULD WE?
WHY CAN'T YOU GIVE MY DAD A JOB?

hood memories of poverty and his sojourn into the real worker's world instilled within him a deep concern for society's problems.

After his inauguration Olson continued to walk a tightrope between his own farmer-labor convictions and what he thought Minnesotans would tolerate. Those who believed that Olson would exhibit radicalism once he took office were sorely disappointed. Olson's recommendations to the legislature reflected his middle-ground position. Although his call for the abolition of injunctions in labor disputes clearly linked him to labor, most of his proposals — conservation, increased highway construction, tax reform, securities sales regulation — seemed to be in the political mainstream and, even, recalled progressive proposals of twenty-five years earlier. Olson avoided direct confrontations with the legislature and seemed pleased that it responded with a $15,000,000 highway program which would employ many workers and a reorganization of the state's conservation efforts.

During the months following the 1931 session Olson took more heat from his own party than from Republicans and Democrats. Some chided him for being too conservative, but his fellow partisans were most upset because he was not cleaning out Republicans and Democrats from appointive offices. Dependent upon Republican and Democratic votes, Olson continued to move slowly in spite of party protest.

The deepening economic crisis, however, forced Olson into bolder action. By late 1931 and throughout 1932, Minnesotans were beginning to feel the terrible onslaught of depression. State-wide unemployment reached 20 percent — on the Range a staggering 70 percent and farm prices plummeted. City streets teemed with the unemployed; factories came to a standstill; banks folded; farmers marched under the banner of the Farmers' Holiday Association, demanding immediate action and threatening to strike. The Farmer-Labor convention in late March 1932 took place in an atmosphere of impending catastrophe.

The convention moved the party gently toward the left. The Farmer-Labor platform called for the placing of water and electric utilities under state control; this kept the party radicals happy. Three proposals attacked the problem of depression: unemployment insurance, old age pension, and an income tax which would place a greater burden on higher incomes. As in 1930, Olson pursued the middle ground during the campaign, attempting to lure Republican and Democratic votes. A primary fight ruptured the Democratic party with energetic John E. Regan emerging as the party's candidate for governor, and Republican candidate Earle Brown tried to pull together his splintered party. During the campaign Olson attacked Brown and the Republican party as

Child pickets, 1937.

JUSTICE
UNITE
120
FREE
SCOTTSBORO BOYS
MACHINISTS · AUTO MECHANICS ·
ORNAMENTAL METAL WORKERS
ADEQUATE CLOTHING FOR ALL YOUNG UNEMPLOYED WORKERS
FIGHT DONT STARVE ORGANIZE
Coca-Cola

Workers and farmers plea for relief on the capitol grounds, 1935.

representatives of the vested interests. "Throughout my entire political career," he declared, "I have been fighting against the forces of reaction and of special privilege." Singling out his Republican opponent, he charged that "Brown can never escape the fact that the people with whom he has had social and business contact all his life are a part of the group which has caused the present economic situation." Brown promised the voters budget reductions and a business-like approach to government. Late in the campaign the Republicans accused the Farmer-Labor party of waging a smear campaign. According to Ray P. Chase, whom Olson had soundly defeated two years before who was running in 1932 for Congress, Olson's supporters had sent a drunken imposter to parade around the state as Brown in order to discredit the Republican. This, along with allegations that Brown was a member of the Ku Klux Klan, was emphatically denied by Republican headquarters. With the economic crisis deepening, the Governor won an easy re-election, polling 522,438 votes; the combined Brown-Regan total was 503,932. The people wanted action to fight the economic plague which was upon them.

Olson's address to the 1933 legislature reflected both his frustration with the inaction of the Hoover administration and his own concern for the plight of his fellow Minnesotans. "Just beyond the horizon is rampant lawlessness and possible revolution," he warned. "Only remedial social legislation . . . can prevent its appearance." To help farmers save their farms, he proposed a scheme of mortgage adjustments and a two-year period between delinquency and foreclosure. For labor he set forth an unemployment insurance plan and again called for the end of injunctions in labor disputes. Taxes on chain stores would aid small businessmen and raise much-needed state revenues. He demanded higher taxes on corporations, a constitutional amendment which would facilitate state development of power, and increased state involvement in relief.

A coalition of farmer-laborites and progressives from the other parties gave the liberals a slim majority in the House, but the Senate remained in conservative hands. Economic collapse stalked Minnesota as the legislature met during the first months of 1933. Angry farmers marched on St. Paul; unemployed workers picketed the capitol building; bank failures became daily occurrences. In spite of recurring ulcers and a bothersome appendix, which was later removed, Olson decided to take the legislature head-on in a determined effort to gain approval for his proposals. The calm and reasonable approach of 1931 turned into a fiery, almost abusive attack in 1933. Driven by what he saw as economic injustice and human suffering, Olson used every means possible to achieve legislative approval for his program. He lashed out against obstructionist conservatives; from the steps of the capitol he harangued timid legislators;

he threatened to declare martial law. Cajoled by an enraged Governor and an angry population, the legislature gave Olson several pieces of legislation: a $2,000,000 direct relief fund, the removal of municipal debt limits, a farm mortgage moratorium, an income tax, a chain-store tax, homestead tax reductions, prohibition of injunctions in labor disputes, tighter regulation of securities and banking, and the beginning of an old-age pension plan. Although the legislature rejected unemployment insurance, it provided Minnesota with its most liberal legislation since the progressive era and gave the state weapons to use in the battle against the depression.

After the repeal of prohibition Olson called a special session of the legislature in early December 1933 to write liquor legislation. At the same time, he took the opportunity to pry additional relief funds from the legislature, proposing that $5,000,000, which would be raised largely through liquor taxes, be used for relief of needy Minnesotans. "You and I have a great opportunity, here and now," he told the legislature, "to make a lasting contribution to the relief of citizens of this state and to the promotion of the common welfare." The legislature, however, balked at the thought of more money for relief; A.J. Rockne, conservative senator and well-to-do farmer and publisher from Zumbrota, fought Olson's scheme and countered with a plan for $500,000 in loans. After two weeks of stalemate, Olson went on the radio to arouse public opinion, bitterly criticizing Rockne as "The Apostle of Reaction." Public pressure forced the legislature to pass Olson's bill, giving Minnesota essential funds to supplement New Deal relief efforts.

Although the economy continued to sag as Minnesotans entered 1934, Governor Olson was optimistic. Federal relief began to brighten the horizon; he had forced the legislature to knuckle under to many of his demands; his Farmer-Labor party seemed to hold a firm grip on Minnesota. When the party's convention convened in March, Olson exuded confidence. He opened the convention with an address which affirmed his concern with "human welfare rather than with selfish privilege . . . with the conservation of the life, happiness, and the security of our citizens." His speech sketched, in vague terms, the need to move toward cooperative enterprises sometime in the future. For the most part, he spoke with restraint and without offensive radicalism. For whatever reason he concluded his address with what farmer-laborites interpreted as a call to arms:

> *Now, I am frank to say that I am not a liberal. I enjoy working on a common basis with liberals for their platforms, etc., but I am not a liberal. I am what I want to be. I am a radical. I am a radical in the sense that I want a definite change in the system. I am not satisfied with tinkering. I am not satisfied with patching. I am not satisfied with hanging a laurel wreath upon burglars and thieves and*

Farmers dramatize the need for relief on the capitol steps, 1935.

pirates and calling them code authorities or something else. I am not satisfied with that.

I want, however, an orderly, a sane and a constructive change. I don't want any more visionary things any more than the hardest tory conservative want [sic] it, but I know the transition can take place and that of course it must be gradual.

Although he spoke in terms of gradual transitions and orderly, sane change, the crowd roared its approval. To them, Olson had confirmed his radicalism, and it became their duty to facilitate that radicalism. In 1930 and 1932 he had carefully controlled the writing of the party platform; in 1934 he left that to the convention and departed for Washington, D.C. immediately after his address. Taking Olson at his word, the convention pushed the party to the radical left through a platform that demanded a "cooperative commonwealth" to be achieved immediately through public ownership of banks, mines, utilities, transportation, and factories. The "cooperative commonwealth" was the rank-and-file farmer-laborites' response to the depression; to them, the old system could not be patched up. With Olson on the train headed for the nation's capital, the party gave him the most radical platform in Minnesota's history.

Olson and the party leaders, who soon had second thoughts about the abrupt shift to the left, spent the ensuing months attempting to turn stark socialism into something which voters could swallow. The Governor maneuvered into a new position, averring that only idle factories, which would manufacture goods for the needy, would fall under the control of the state. This, he argued, was "completely Christian and American." In May the party leadership issued a revised platform which played down the "cooperative commonwealth" and advanced the Governor's "idle factory scheme" along with the more traditional unemployment insurance, farm mortgage moratoriums, and tax reform.

Throughout the campaign, however, Republican Martin Nelson, an attorney from Austin, and Democrat John Regan relentlessly tied Olson to radicalism. A.C. Townley, who entered the race as an independent, attacked Olson as a political opportunist who had turned against his own party's convictions in order to get votes. Olson countered these attacks from the left and the right with a campaign in which he cast himself as the champion of the common man and the defender of the people against an unfair system: "We charge that it fails utterly to meet the needs of our people; that the massive load of misery and suffering which we witness all about us is due to its inherent defects." Although the combined votes of his opponents exceeded his by 110,000, Olson defeated his nearest challenger by 72,000: Olson, 468,812; Nelson, 396,359; Regan, 176,928;

The People's Lobby takes a coffee break, 1937.

Townley, 4,454. Olson had been re-elected, but the ghost of radicalism haunted the Farmer-Labor party.

The election wrecked the liberal control of the House; conservatives held a firm grip on the 1935 legislature. Rockne and other anti-Olsonites relished the opportunity to strike back at the Governor. The Senate launched investigations into the highway and relief agencies, hoping to discredit Olson with discoveries of widespread graft and corruption. The probes created bold headlines and stirred the political pot but did little else. The Senate did support appropriations but adamantly refused to pass other Olson proposals. Plagued by stomach trouble throughout the session, Olson seemed to lose much of his punch in battling the legislature.

By fall the Governor had decided to run against U.S. Senator Thomas A. Schall, a staunchly conservative Republican. This raised the question of who would succeed Olson as governor. Lieutenant Governor Hjalmer Petersen, a country editor from Askov, saw himself as the logical heir apparent. Party insiders, however, boosted Commissioner of Banking Elmer Benson. In late December Senator Schall was struck and killed by a car, giving Olson the chance to appoint a replacement. Olson ruled out self-appointment and personally favored the selection of his former aide, Judge Vince Day. Before the Governor could act, however, the *Minnesota Leader,* without Olson's knowledge, announced that Elmer Benson would be appointed to the Senate seat. Behind-the-scenes manuevering by a coterie of Benson-for-Governor partisans had forced Olson to appoint their man, giving him the inside track for the gubernatorial nomination. To maintain party unity, Olson named Benson, who then announced that he would serve out Schall's term and step aside for Olson in the forthcoming election.

Benson had barely packed his bags when news hit the streets that Governor Olson had been hospitalized in Rochester for a stomach tumor. The surgeons informed Olson and the public that removal of the tumor was inadvisable and that x-ray treatment was best. Few Minnesotans had the impression that he was in danger. Olson spent some of the winter in Arizona and returned for the March 1936 Farmer-Labor convention. Although he had lost considerable weight, the Governor entered fully into the drafting of a platform and delivered a powerful address in which he called for government ownership of plants which made arms and ammunition for war: "It is as unwise to permit private enterprise to manufacture and sell armaments and munitions for war to the government, as it would be for the Government of the United States to hire mercenary armies to fight its battle for it."

Patriotism — even in a time of despair, Rochester, 1937.

Although Lieutenant Governor Petersen knew that Senator Benson had the nomination for governor, he made a fight for it anyway. A month before the convention he had spoken out publicly against the leadership of the party. "Our party is sorely in need of discipline," he declared, "and that I shall provide, that will be my personal ambition." If he were to become governor, he promised that "the half-dozen 'Mexican generals' in the party will work and spend far less time on their selfish political patronage, conniving, and fixing. They will be put in place." At the convention Petersen warned that "any political party that resorts chiefly to steamroller tactics and patronage is doomed to failure, sooner or later." Unruffled, Benson confidently responded, "Our opponents will achieve victory if victory can be achieved with gold. And they will furnish the thirty pieces of silver to any Judas who wants to betray us." Petersen's followers tried to convince the convention to nominate two men and to let the people decide in the primary. The convention, however, overwhelmingly rejected the proposal and nominated Benson. A disappointed Petersen was given the nomination for Railroad and Warehouse Commissioner as a consolation prize. The party platform had a vaguely socialistic ring, but attempts to add specific public ownership schemes were soundly defeated. The party had learned from the fiasco of two years earlier.

Although Olson's weight had dropped to 130 pounds by April, he still was able to make appearances and plan campaign strategy. President Roosevelt was worried that Olson's party might align itself with a national third-party movement — the Union party — which might cause the President trouble in Minnesota. In a secret deal Olson promised support for Roosevelt if the Democratic candidates for senator and governor would withdraw from the race shortly before the election. Olson knew that the Farmer-Labor party faced a tough battle — especially in the light of his narrower victory of 1934. This, he thought, would ensure victory.

During most of the summer Olson shuttled back and forth between Gull Lake and Rochester with stop-offs at the capitol, and his campaign appearances became infrequent. Party insiders began to whisper about his possible withdrawal from the race and even his resignation from the governorship. On August 12 Lieutenant Governor Petersen, still smarting from the convention's rebuff, wrote to Olson, revealing privately his deep-seated displeasure with the party. He resented the Governor's appointment of "crown prince Elmer" to the Senate and scolded Olson for breaking his "hospital-room" promise to "pass out the word" in the party "to endorse two for the governorship." By not waging a bitter floor fight at the convention, Petersen was certain that he had saved the party: "Had the fight taken place the eyes of many would have been opened and it is

Farmers crowd into St. Paul to demand help, 1935.

very possible that the esteem in which you are held might have been lessened considerably, and certainly Elmer could have been made to look thirty cents." If Olson were to withdraw and resign because of illness, he could "square the account" with Petersen "by arranging it so that Elmer becomes the candidate for the Senate and that I become the candidate for Governor." Ten days later Olson died.

As Minnesotans mourned the loss of their governor, the party committee chose Congressman Ernest Lundeen to replace Olson on the ticket. To Benson, the campaign was a "clash between darkness and enlightenment." Benson embarked on an energetic, whirlwind campaign, haranguing Republican candidate Martin Nelson as a reactionary who was anti-labor, anti-farmer, and even anti-school children. Nelson painted Benson as an ultra-radical and called for tax relief: "Elmer, your party is fluent with promises and bombastic with words, but its tax record is a tragic farce." At the propitious time, the Democractic candidates withdrew. Benson and Lundeen easily won the election — Benson by 225,000 votes, three times Olson's 1934 margin. "The rule of dog eat dog, the jungle law of rugged individualism, is at an end," declared Benson. "We are on the road to a happier society."

The forty-one year old Benson brought a much different background to the governorship than had Olson. Benson had grown up in the small town of Appleton in Swift County, where his father owned a successful general store and farm. After high school he studied and later practiced law in St. Paul. After World War I he returned to Appleton to work as a bank cashier, and during the 1920s he became one of the few bankers to sympathize with the Nonpartisan League. When Floyd B. Olson asked him to become Commissioner of Securities in the new Farmer-Labor administration, Benson eagerly accepted the opportunity. Olson's confidence in Benson became apparent in April 1933, when the Governor named the Appleton native to the post of Commissioner of Banking. Although Commissioner Benson had not been Olson's first choice to fill Schall's vacant Senate seat, the Governor showed no great displeasure over the maneuver which brought Benson the position. While he served his brief tenure in Washington, Senator Benson earned a reputation as a fighter for liberal causes.

Disregarding the conservatives who still controlled the Senate, Benson tossed caution aside and laid out a comprehensive Farmer-Labor program to the 1937 legislature. The Governor explained that the depression had altered the nature of government. It no longer was just the protector of private property; it now had become provider of social and economic security for all people. Minnesotans, according to Benson, wanted a liberal program consistent with the expanded function of government. He demanded the

WPA - refurbished toys cheered most youngsters, St. Paul.

lowering of the legal interest rate to four percent, registration of lobbyists, labor safety legislation, extension of the farm-mortgage moratorium, a tax on chain-farming, creation of a public housing agency, union pay for state employees, increased workman's compensation benefits, a teacher tenure law, state-funded youth projects, expansion of city-owned power boundaries, more funding for old-age pensions and welfare, and state-owned power plants, liquor stores, and cement plant. The Governor hoped to finance these expanded government services by reforming the tax structure. He insisted upon significantly higher taxes on wealth — iron ore and telephone, insurance, railroad, and electric companies.

Each day of the legislative session brought a new crisis for the Governor. The House would pass Benson-supported tax legislation, and the Senate would kill it. Throughout the winter months, Benson continually attacked the conservative Senate in special messages, radio broadcasts, and face-to-face confrontations. "I ask those conservative senators who are so loyally championing the cause of the steel trust to examine the matter in the light of the welfare of the State as a whole," he chided. "May I point out to them that our iron ore resources are the natural heritage of the people." When the Senate would not budge, he encouraged a people's lobby to force the Senate into action. In early April several hundred farmers and workers marched on the Capitol to invade the legislative chambers. The liberal House listened attentively to their concerns, but the conservative Senate adjourned and scurried for shelter. The Senate Tax Committee, however, did not escape the lobby's anger. The throng found the Committee and drove it from its meeting room with a barrage of jeers. The lobby had no impact on the Senate and made Farmer-Laborites appear lawless. Conference committees failed; Benson's personal appearances did no good; the House and Senate remained deadlocked. On April 21 the session ended; most of Benson's proposals had failed, and Minnesota still had no tax program.

Governor Benson had no alternative but to call a special session. Through the hot summer of 1937 the session plodded on with little result. The House and the Governor held out for $38,602,260 in new revenue which he believed to be essential to support depression programs; the Senate refused to go above $6,401,260. Benson kept a tight rein on the House to make sure that it would not buckle. Tired of the continuous warfare, however, the House, in a weak moment, compromised with the Senate: $14,377,260 in new revenue. Benson was outraged and refused to sign the measure, allowing it to become law without his signature.

WPA tailors make clothes for the needy, Minneapolis, 1936.

Benson's fight over taxing wealthy companies caused friction with not only the business community but also his own party members who thought he was too inflexible. Olson had been a master of holding divergent groups together; Benson was not. Believing that his victory of 1936 had been a mandate for immediate change, he stubbornly held to his ideas of what needed to be done, refusing to compromise.

During his term as governor, Benson stirred one controversy after another. Imbued with a zealous crusading spirit, he was not afraid to step on toes, even those of his own party loyalists. During 1937 he took vehemently strong stands in support of labor. In August he participated in a New York City rally sponsored by the League Against War and Fascism. Benson delivered a scathing attack on fascism and urged militant farmers and workers to unite across the land. In December he went to California to give the main address at a rally to free labor-leader Tom Mooney, who was serving prison time for bombing a Preparedness Day celebration in 1916. Benson challenged all Americans to take up Mooney's cause and denounced those who had put labor's spokesman behind bars. At home he took the side of workers in disputes with management. By the end of 1937 few Minnesotans held a neutral view of Elmer Benson.

Opposition to Benson did not come only from business, Republicans, and other conservatives. Within his own party, discord turned into open rebellion in 1938, when Hjalmer Petersen, irked with Benson and his "Mexican generals," filed as a candidate for governor two months prior to the March convention. In 1936 he had written to a friend in California that he had not disrupted the party with a nomination fight because he was "too much of a party man." Believing that the party had gone too far to the left and that party leaders had treated him with disdain, he abandoned his 1936 position. During the weeks before the convention, he wrote to party members throughout Minnesota, attempting to round up enough support for the nomination. Petersen openly criticized Governor Benson, charging that his administration had squandered tax money and had catered to communists. On February 12 Benson came out swinging against conservatives, among whom he counted Petersen, who were "throwing dust in the eyes of the taxpayers." "The slaughter of liberal measures," Benson quipped about the 1937 legislature, "would have set a record for the South St. Paul stockyard." He reminded his audience that the Farmer-Labor party's goal was "to bring the greatest good to the greatest number . . . raising the living standards of our people, to free them from the nightmare of social and economic insecurity."

Hjalmer Petersen chats with reporters, 1936.

When the March convention endorsed Governor Benson, Petersen bolted and entered the primary. The vicious battle split the party wide-open as the two jockeyed for

votes. Petersen struck out at Benson's radicalism, insinuating that the Governor was linked to the communist movement. Benson classed his opponent as a conservative and continued his call for a "real modification of our economic system which will bring about a more equitable distribution of wealth and income." The election was close; challenger Petersen carried 51 counties to Benson's 36, but the Governor won nomination by 16,000 votes.

The Republicans selected the thirty-one-year-old Harold E. Stassen, state's attorney from South St. Paul, to face Benson in the general election. The youthful Stassen presented himself as one who could rescue Minnesota from the "political and economic quagmire" into which the Farmer-Labor party had plunged the state. He waged a positive campaign in which he pledged voters that he could carry out many of the Farmer-Labor programs but would do so with business sense and honesty. At the Becker County fair he promised to extend old-age assistance and to maintain relief; in Hibbing he told workers that he would appoint a commission to devise methods of relieving unemployment on the Range; in St. Paul he supported a civil service reform bill and vowed that "petty political conniving and card holding in a political party will not be a requirement of public service." He courted labor's vote in the Twin Cities, asserting that "I believe that in the building up of a state a sound labor relations policy is the firmest step that can be taken," and that "the arm of the state should never be used to crush labor." The Farmer-Labor party became so concerned with Stassen's successful image as a liberal that it widely distributed a cartoon flier which depicted Stassen at a microphone shouting, "I am a liberal." Behind him stood three fat, formally-dressed men labeled packing trust, steel trust, and utilities, laughing, "Haw, Haw, Haw."

Although Stassen resisted red-baiting techniques in his personal remarks, other Republicans did not. The Republicans sponsored a series of radio programs on which "Farmer-Labor supporters" branded Benson as a communist. "The communistic agents of Stalin and Trotsky saw in the labor unions and the Farmer-Labor party, fertile soil in which to practice their principles and doctrines," claimed Ralph Carmean, a unionist. He went on to say that Hjalmer Petersen and the "founders of the Farmer-Labor party" were supporting Stassen "because he has assured them that he will give them a square deal. And they need not be Communists to get it."

The *Minneapolis Journal* was representative of the newspaper opposition when it told its readers that "the official Communist party has been active at all times in support of Governor Benson, in shaping his platform at Duluth, in getting him the Farm-Labor nomination, and in the campaign for his re-election." The most damaging and damning

Young Harold Stassen politics with folks during Sauerkraut Days in Henderson, 1937.

Fresh Taystee
BREA
PURITY BA
7-36
SERIAL NO.
CHEERIO GIN

denouncement of Benson came in a 60-page pamphlet entitled "Are They Communists or Catspaws?" written by Ray P. Chase, who did not hide the intent of his work by subtitling it "A Red Baiting Article." Chase filled the pamphlet with reproductions of photographs and documents which linked Benson with communists. "A Communist is defined," Chase explained, "in *The Northwest Communist* of February 1, 1938, p. 4, col. 1, in the leading editorial: 'Benson: No. 1 Labor Governor.'" Page after page "documented" Benson's radicalism and "Communist connections." Chase warned Benson that "Hysterical screams of Red Baiting! Red Baiting! will not be an adequate answer."

Benson categorically denied that he was a communist and emphatically avowed his disdain for dictatorship, describing the red scare as a Republican smokescreen to cover up a reactionary philosophy. The "Working Newspapermen's Benson Volunteer Committee" attempted to counter what it termed "the witch hunt of 1938" in a pamphlet entitled "Deadline!" "Newspapermen know bigotry is a weapon of political reaction," it affirmed. "We believe in the fight for democracy as reflected in the progressive liberalism of Governor Elmer A. Benson." Benson and his supporters, however, could do little to convince voters that the Governor was the victim of a red scare; and Petersen refused to endorse Benson. Stassen soundly defeated him at the polls, 680,342 to 387,263. Only one Farmer-Labor candidate for state or federal office survived the landslide. Minnesota had repudiated the Farmer-Labor party.

The debacle of 1938 closed a chaotic chapter in Minnesota political history. The Farmer-Labor coalition fell apart. It is unlikely that even Floyd B. Olson could have kept it together; certainly Elmer Benson could not. Unrest among farmers and workingmen during the 1920s and the depression of the 1930s, coupled with the personal appeal of Olson, made possible the success of the Farmer-Labor party. By 1938, in part due to Farmer-Labor programs, the pain of the depression had subsided. Crop yields and farm prices were better; unemployment was not as severe; business was on the upswing. Minnesota's mood had become more conservative. Then, too, the Farmer-Labor years had been filled with upheaval and political bickering; the people had grown weary of squabble and deadlock, and Harold Stassen and his youth had wide-spread appeal to a population yearning for a fresh start. In 1938 he promised what Olson had in 1930: a new approach to old problems.

During the 1930s Minnesotans — like the nation as a whole — wanted change, but not revolution. They favored Farmer-Labor programs which helped take the sting out of the depression: the farm moratorium, homestead tax reductions, old-age pensions, and expanded relief. Their enthusiasm for Farmer-Labor leadership cooled quickly when the

WPA workers recycle toys for Christmas, St. Paul.

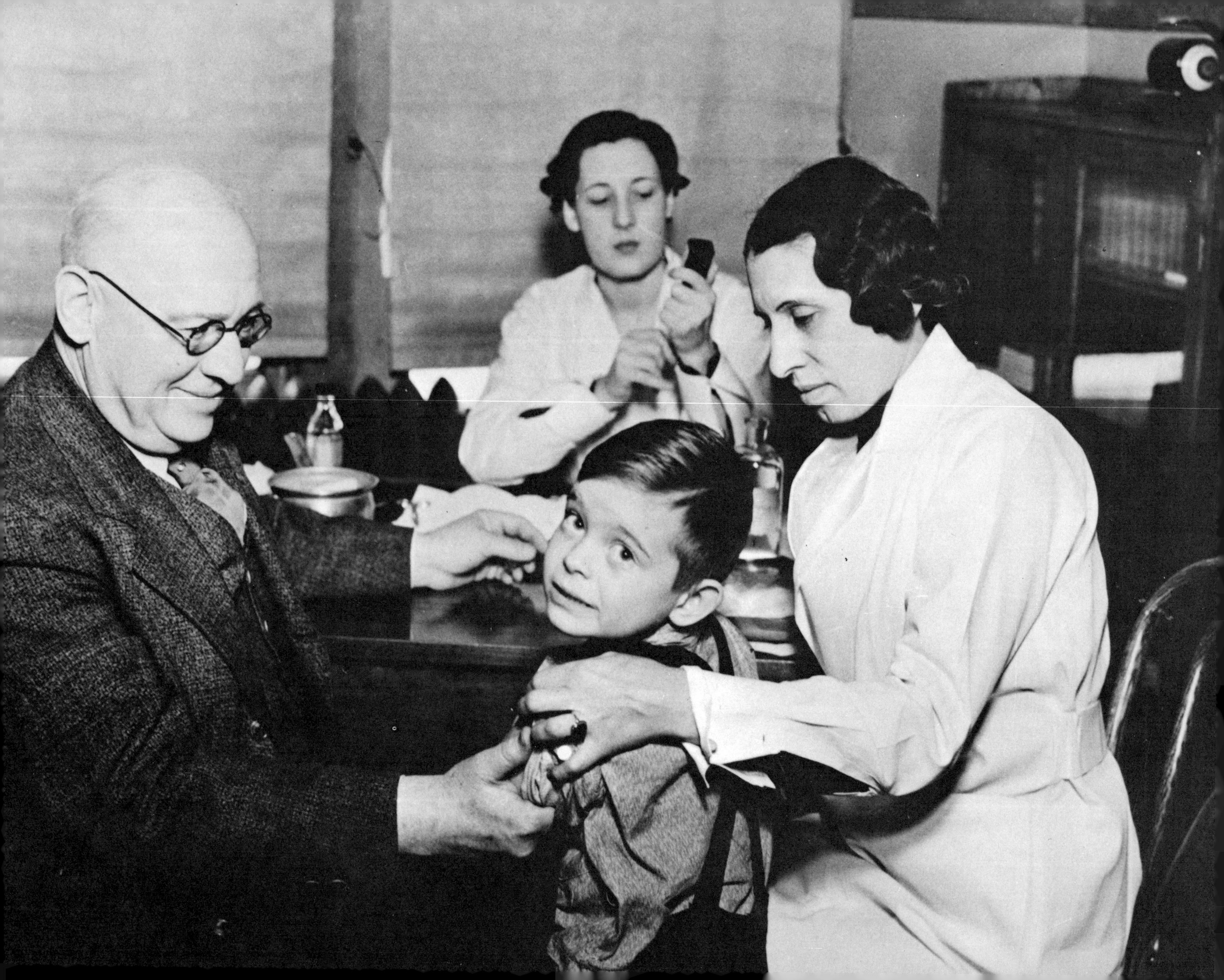

party began to espouse a "cooperative commonwealth" and when Benson argued for "social ownership." The Olson-Benson years, however, moved Minnesota toward the political left. Stassen dared not repudiate reforms which the Farmer-Labor party had initiated because he knew that he, like Olson, depended upon broad support. The Republican party that controlled Minnesota for so many years after 1939 practiced a brand of progressive Republicanism, reflecting a stance into which the depression and the Farmer-Labor party had forced it.

WPA health unit in St. Paul.

BIBLIOGRAPHICAL ESSAY

Four manuscript collections at the Minnesota Historical Society are indispensible for anyone who wishes to profile the 1930s. The Ray Park Chase papers contain valuable materials on banking trends and, because of his centrality to Republican politics, the Minnesota Republican party. The Floyd Bjornstjerne Olson collection is small and contains very little of Olson's correspondence. Several speeches and press releases, however, provide the flavor of his politics. Of much more value to an understanding of the Farmer-Labor party, especially the internal struggles, are the papers of Elmer Austin Benson and Hjalmer Petersen.

Two histories of Minnesota furnish solid overviews of the 1930s: Theodore C. Blegen (with a concluding chapter by Russell W. Fridley), *Minnesota: A History of the State* (Minneapolis, 1975) and William E. Lass, *Minnesota: A Bicentennial History* (New York, 1977). The politics of the decade deserves more scholarship than it has received. George

Happy faces buried in Big-Little Books, St. Cloud, 1939.

H. Mayer, *The Political Career of Floyd B. Olson* (Minneapolis, 1951) is the standard biography of Olson. James M. Shields, *Mr. Progressive: A Biography of Elmer Austin Benson* (Minneapolis, 1971) presents Governor Benson in a very favorable light and contains useful information which can be found nowhere else. Millard L. Gieske, *Minnesota Farmer-Laborites: The Third Party Alternative* (Minneapolis, 1979) is a detailed and scholarly study of the farmer-labor coalition. Two works give valuable background in political history: Carl H. Chrislock, *The Progressive Era in Minnesota, 1899-1918* (St. Paul, 1971) and Robert L. Morlan, *Political Prairie Fire: The Non-partisan League, 1915-1922 (Minneapolis, 1955).*

Three articles provide astute insights into the difficulties which Minnesota workers faced during the depression: Thomas E. Blantz, "Father Hass and the Minneapolis Truckers' Strike of 1934," Minnesota History 42 (Spring, 1970), 5-15; Herman Erickson, "WPA Strike and Trials of 1939," *Minnesota History* 42 (Summer, 1971), 202-214; Larry D. Engelmann, "'We Were the Poor People.' The Hormel Strike of 1933," *Labor History* 15 (Fall, 1974), 483-510.

Don W. Larson, *Land of the Giants: A History of Minnesota Business* (Minneapolis, 1979) is a readable popular history which has sound information on banking and business during the 1930s. Doniver A. Lund, *A History of First National Bank of St. Peter, Minnesota* (St. Peter, 1967) contains an excellent section on the problems of a small bank.

The impact of the depression on the "plain people" is discussed in three studies: John L. Shover, *Cornbelt Rebellion: The Farmers' Holiday Association* (Urbana, 1965); George Tselos, "Self-Help and Sauerkraut: The Organized Unemployed, Inc. of Minneapolis," *Minnesota History* 45 (Winter 1977), 306-320: Calvin W. Gower, "The CCC Indian Division: Aid for Depressed Americans, 1933-1945," *Minnesota History* (Spring, 1972), 3-13.

Several newspapers provided information and editorial comment on specific events: The *St. Paul Pioneer Press,* the *Minneapolis Journal,* the *Grand Forks Herald,* the *New York Times, and the Worthington Globe.*

The deluge of statistics are derived from hundreds of government reports (WPA, FERA, AAA, NYA, CCC, CWA, PWA, FSA, the census). They tend to be dull but are essential to the profile.

Winona women on a WPA recreation program.

ACKNOWLEDGMENTS

Austin children enjoy a WPA recreation program.

Ten years ago Dan Rylance, archivist at the University of North Dakota, and I thought that the story of North Dakota's depression years ought to be told. *Years of Despair: North Dakota and the Depression* (1972) resulted from our collaboration. Shortly thereafter, Moorhead State University invited us to teach a course which covered Minnesota and the Dakotas during the depression era. In that course Minnesota became my focus, and I began the process of thinking through Minnesota's uniqueness as it confronted the 1930s. Five years ago a historian-friend, who has requested that he go unnamed, asked me to write a lengthy essay on depression Minnesota for a book which was to profile representative states. I completed my essay, but alas, the others did not. The book never materialized. One day I was recounting this sad tale to Archer Jones, Director of the North Dakota Institute for Regional Studies. He asked to see my manuscript and agreed to publish Minnesota's depression story. Therefore, I wish to thank Dan Rylance for

POT
PUT
TAKE
GUM

sharpening my focus on the depression, my unnamed friend for convincing me to write about Minnesota and Archer Jones for liking the essays.

I appreciate very much the assistance that others have given me. Thomas Howard and William Gard, both of the Department of History in the University of North Dakota, and Bill Reid of North Dakota State University's Department of History read and made valuable suggestions about the essays. The Minnesota Historical Society Staff in the manuscript and the photographic divisions provided courteous and prompt service. I thank the Minnesota Historical Society for granting permission to use the photographs which appear in this book. Carol Taylor and Liz Hamill typed and proofed the manuscript with skill and patience. Lastly, I deeply appreciate the inspiration and help given me through the years by my colleague and friend Robert P. Wilkins.

Minneapolis authorities fight gambling, 1932. The photographs which appear on the next seven pages illustrate the cheer which WPA projects brought to Minnesotans.

EVERY - ONE
ENJOYS
PERFECT MUSIC
IS OURS
PERFECT?

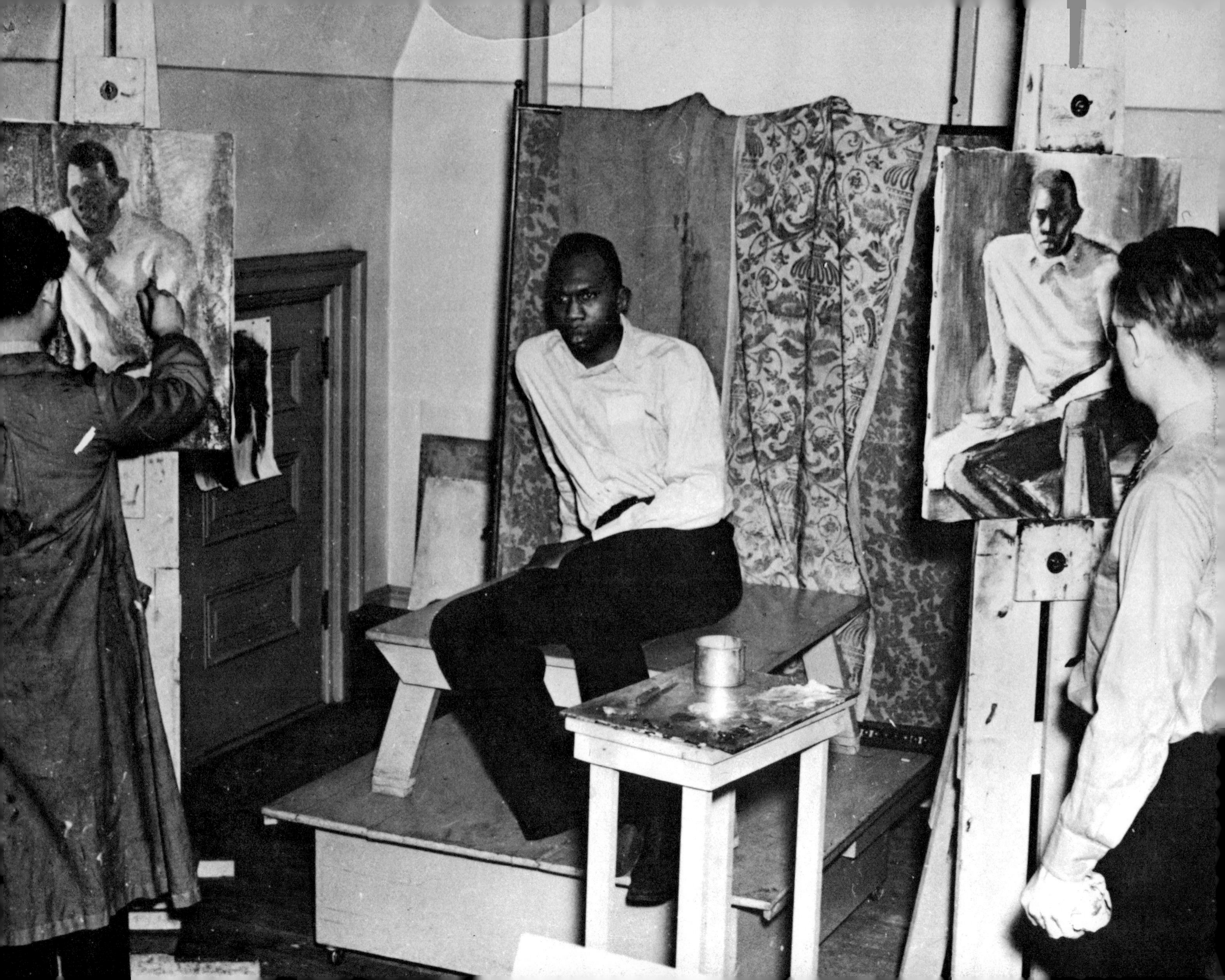

INDEX